IMAGES
of Scotland
AROUND CALLANDER
AND THE
TROSSACHS

Compiled by
Morag Lloyds

TEMPUS

First published 1999
Copyright © Morag Lloyds, 1999

Tempus Publishing Limited
The Mill, Brimscombe Port,
Stroud, Gloucestershire, GL5 2QG

ISBN 0 7524 1082 2

Typesetting and origination by
Tempus Publishing Limited
Printed in Great Britain by
Midway Clark Printing, Wiltshire

00576 3284

This book is dedicated to my son Allan.

914.136

Contents

Foreword

The area of Scotland known as the Trossachs is an area with great natural beauty, fascinating history, the glamour of legends, and an appeal which draws people to it even in the sophisticated world of today.

There is an enormous attraction for people in being able to get away from the pressure of the present moment and to find a place to relax and reflect. The Trossachs and the villages and towns which surround it have provided that opportunity for many years. Wherever you go there are wonderful places to pause, panoramas to thrill, and a long history to inspire. We are surrounded by hills and lochs which once echoed the shouts of the clansmen, but today provide recreation for the walker, the climber and those looking for a day out.

We pass through towns and hamlets where we are aware of buildings with character – buildings which have a story to tell of those who lived, worked and visited there. We come across communities where people still remember what things were like in years gone by – and are keen to tell you if you have the time to listen. We cannot travel through the countryside without being conscious of the thread which links us to the past. Yet it is a thread which can be so easily lost or carelessly broken, unless we take the time to protect and look after it. It needs someone to note it down, record it and make it available to those who have an interest in enhancing the present with the heritage of the past. Morag Lloyds has been able to do exactly that with this visual record of one of the most visited parts of the country.

Life inevitably involves change. Change is carved on the face of our communities and our countryside if we are sensitive enough to look for it. Change is as much a part of this area of Scotland as anywhere else – but this is what makes this book particularly interesting. We can see how things have developed, where there has been growth and decline, how people used to live, and what took their time, attention and interest in years gone by. We can understand something of their values in life and what mattered most. We live in a world which seems to move very quickly, where transport and entertainment, education and recreation, are all so readily available. It is hard for us to imagine what life was like for those who walked and travelled these roads before us. This book helps us to imagine, and in so doing it strengthens the thread with the past.

A glance through the following pages will undoubtedly enrich for us the present, because so much of our enjoyment of this place has to do with history, its characters and the place it has held in the hearts of many down through the centuries. It has a well-deserved reputation, and if this book is able to help us appreciate even more the countryside and communities which make up and neighbour the Trossachs, then it will have done what the author set out to do.

Revd Iain M. Goring
Callander Kirk, 1999

Introduction

I have lived on and off in this area for the past thirty-six years, and I have seen many changes both in Callander and the surrounding villages where people no longer live off the land but commute each day to towns and cities.

New faces and new ways have brought a different way of life to the area, but in the process the knowledge of many old traditions and the local social history is in danger of being lost forever.

It is not my belief that people are not interested, far from it, when I have attended local antique fairs with my old postcards, the interest is overwhelming. All of you that I have met and chatted to at these fairs will note that the vast amount of information passed to me was not wasted – many thanks to you all!

I hope that many will find something here of interest to them and perhaps look a little differently at the view outside their window.

Acknowledgements

I have tried to be as accurate as humanely possible with times, dates and names, but to err is human. My apologies for any inadvertent omissions of attribution.

Firstly, my thanks to the Revd Iain Goring, Callander Kirk, for writing the foreword to this book. Special thanks to Dr N. Reid of the Department of Manuscripts at the Valentine archive in St Andrews University for his kind permission to reproduce a number of their postcards, Whiteholmes of Dundee for their kind permission in also reproducing several of their postcards, and to the following who have given me help in a variety of ways:
John Brims, George Dixon and Peter Clapham of Stirling District Archives, who were invaluable at retrieving obscure information with good humour, Kay Dickson of the Scottish Pottery Society, Ken Dunn MBE, Harvey McNaughton, Hugh McDiarmid, Catriona Oldham (nee Ferguson), Robin McLean, Jean Fail (nee Campbell), Betty Beauchamp, Dick Reevie, Mrs Love, Elizabeth Morton, Mary Mathieson, the late Jock Innes, Elma Beagrie, David Hirst, Ronnie and Jimmy Gibson, Catherine and Fred Manzies, and Matthew Forlow of Tempus Publishing for his incredible patience, help and good humour. Finally, thank you to the many people, friends and family who have given me the encouragement and put up with so much – here at last is the book!

One

Aberfoyle and
the Trossachs

W.M.Watt's shop sold stationery and picture postcards, and in fact published many early views of the Trossachs. The shop was situated next to the Railway Square and was eventually taken over by Frame's the bootmakers.

A view of the beautiful 'Lake of Menteith', the only 'lake' in Scotland.

These are the ruins of the Augustinian Priory of Inchmahome (once spelt *Inchmaguhomok*, meaning the Isle of Rest) which date back to the middle of the thirteenth century. The island stands at the north end of the Lake of Menteith. Amongst the famous visitors to the Priory are Robert the Bruce and the young Mary Queen of Scots, who stayed on the Island with her mother for just under three weeks following the Battle of Pinkie. The island of Inchmahome once had orchards and at one time or another a granary, brewhouse, bakehouse and an infirmary. In 1926, the Duke of Montrose gave the guardianship of the Priory to the Commissioners of HM Works.

10

Aberfoyle main street, *c.* 1900. There was once an iron market in Aberfoyle which lasted to the beginning of this century and many foreign craftsmen were brought in to the district to work the iron. There is also a story that the 'Venetian Master', Andrea Ferrara, made swords in the Trossachs area at the end of the sixteenth century.

Jean McAlpine's inn, *c.* 1910. This is being rebuilt at the moment.

Forest Hills Hotel, *c.* 1930.

View of Aberfoyle. The statistical account (1791–1799) shows there were approximately thirty-eight farmers in the district and sixteen smiths, tailors, shoemakers, weavers, masons and carpenters. The farms grew oats and barley and kept black cattle, sheep and goats. The forest around Aberfoyle was mainly oak. There was a parochial school which taught the rudiments of Latin and two schools for propagating Christian knowledge; one of which taught reading, writing and arithmetic and the other which taught girls to knit and sew. At this time more than half the children died before reaching the age of ten.

The Bailie Nicol Jarvie Hotel, c. 1900, was named after a Glasgow cloth merchant who was also a distant cousin of Rob Roy. In 1891 the proprietor of the hotel was James Blair. An advertisement around this time states that the hotel hired out boats on Loch Ard and Loch Chon for fishing and pleasure, and there was a tennis lawn, railway station, post and telegraph offices within two minutes walk of the hotel. This photograph is about ten years or so later than the advertisement was printed, but it gives an idea as to how tourism was well on its way by this date!

Four-in-hand coach in the Trossachs, 1930. The mode of transport for the tourists in the early part of the century, the four-in-hand coach was used for excursions and general transport in the area.

Loch Ard, *c.* 1940. There once was an ironworks at Duchray Castle on the south side of Loch Ard around the fifteenth century.

INVERSNAID HOTEL, LOCH LOMOND, FROM THE PIER.   B. 1573.

The Inversnaid Hotel, *c.* 1955.

Glengyle House. Glengyle House is the birthplace of Rob Roy, and is the ancient seat of the chiefs of the Clan McGregor. The Duke of Montrose burned the original house to the ground in 1716. It is believed that the new building, which was built in 1728, was erected to the front of the ruin, and over the years this has been extended and changed. The Glasgow Water Board purchased Glengyle House in the 1920s.

Stronachlachar Hotel. The original hotel was built by the Duke of Montrose at the edge of the Loch Katrine, but when the water level was raised by five feet as part of the work for the Glasgow water supply, the Commissioners of the Waterworks had to replace the hotel with a new building around 1890. The proprietor of the new hotel was a Mr Ferguson. Boats with experienced boatmen were available for visitors wanting to fish or just enjoy the peace of the loch. Coaches ran during the summer months to and from Inversnaid to connect with the steamers at Loch Katrine and Loch Lomond and carriages were also available to be hired. At the outbreak of the Second World War, the hotel was no longer open and in 1975 Strathclyde Regional Council took over the building to convert into flats for employees.

Entrance to Glasgow Corporation Waterworks. The Loch Katrine aqueduct was one of the largest works of its kind in the country. Work started in the spring of 1856, and a tunnel was cut into the mountain 6,975 feet in length to take the water to the Loch Chon side. From there it carries on twenty-six miles by aqueducts and tunnels to the reservoir at Mugdock, which contains around 500,000,000 gallons of water to supply the City of Glasgow. The work took three and a half years, employing 3,000 men. The engineer was John Frederic Bateman.

Trossachs Pier, c. 1920.

In the early days of tourism a boat called the *Water Witch*, which had a crew of eight strong men, rowed tourists out to Ellens Isle and the silver strand. In 1843 a small iron steamer called the *Gypsy* was launched on Loch Katrine. It is believed that some of the boatmen saw this boat as a threat to their livelihoods and sank her. Although newspapers at the time who carried the story of the sinking of the *Gypsy* vowed to find the culprits, nothing was ever proven. In 1846, the first *Rob Roy* was launched on Loch Katrine, followed in June 1855 by *Rob Roy II* (which is shown in this photograph).

Sir Walter Scott and *Rob Roy II*. The *Sir Walter Scott* was launched on Loch Katrine on 31 October 1899. She was built by William Denny and Brothers Ltd, Dumbarton and has been sailing on Loch Katrine ever since. The *Rob Roy II* was moored in 1900 by the side of the Trossachs Pier and can be seen again in this photograph.

Loch Achray and Ben Venue. At one time there was an ironworks behind the Loch Achray Hotel and it is believed that a mound in the Achray water is the remains of a cooling dam.

Trossachs New Road.

Trossachs new road. The new road was opened on 5 June 1885 by the Duke of Montrose, who lent the money for the building of the road. The engineer was Mr Charles Forman of the Aberfoyle Slate Company. The Aberfoyle Slate Quarries were once the third largest in Scotland, and at one time around forty houses stood at the entrance to the Quarries and this road, which is now known as the 'Duke's Pass'.

Trossachs church. This church was built in 1849 and the architect was G.P. Kennedy, who trained under Sir Charles Barry (architect of the Houses of Parliament). Mr Kennedy also designed the Trossachs Hotel. Inside the church is a memorial to the soldiers belonging to, or native to the Trossachs, who fell in the First World War. The monument, which was erected in the summer of 1919, is made of teak from the timber of HMS *Britannia*. With a cross of copper, it has eighteen names from a parish of less than 300.

The above photograph shows the famous Trossachs Hotel in its heyday. Between 1852 and 1864, there were two Trossachs Hotels. The other hotel was built in 1852 but burnt down in 1864, and was totally destroyed in the process. The stables were left standing and Andrew Blair took these over, with this building eventually becoming the post office. The old Trossachs Hotel, which is pictured above, was built in 1849, and it is believed that the architect was again G.P. Kennedy. Later, two wings were added, and the building now forms part of a timeshare complex.

Brig O' Turk Village. This view looks up the same road on which both the Tea-room and the Village Hall now stand. To the left of the photograph was the Smithy. Hugh MacGregor was a blacksmith in Brig O' Turk for forty-eight years, and died at Clan Alpine Cottage in 1923 aged eighty-two.

Brig O' Turk. This view above is of a much later date and shows the Tea-room on the left of the photograph and the Village Hall on the right.

Miss Catherine Ferguson or 'Big Kate' as she was also known, was the well-known landlady of the Brig O' Turk Inn, and was born at Lendrick, Loch Vennacher. In her youth she was slim, but as time went by, Kate put on a fair amount of weight. She was always cheerful and kind and was an extremely popular landlady. Queen Victoria, whilst on a visit to Drunky House, in 1868, had heard so much about Kate that she decided to call in on her. Before she left, the Queen presented Kate with a gift of two sovereigns that became Kate's most prized possessions. Kate died in 1872.

Miss Ferguson's inn.

The post office, Brig O' Turk. Mr D. McAdam was the carriage and motor hirer around 1940.

Dundarroch. This is a very handsome house, which sits up behind the Byre Inn in Brig O' Turk. The valuation rolls for 1873-1897 show that a retired ship's captain called James Munro lived in Dundarroch during these years. This photograph is taken around 1940.

Two

Callander and
Kilmahog

Callander Railway Station, *c.* 1885. The railway arrived at Callander in 1858. The original station was at the east end of Callander and was built by the Dunblane, Doune & Callander Railway Company. Another small station was added at the west end, behind the Dreadnought Hotel. However, this station couldn't cope at busy times, so in 1881 the Callander & Oban Railway enlarged it.

The Callander Railway Station Staff, *c.* 1896. Among the staff are Andrew Johnston (Station Master), Mr Robb (Driver), and Duncan Campbell (Porter).

Callander Railway Station, *c.* 1930.

Main Street looking towards Stirling, *c*. 1960, with the bulldozer at an interesting angle.

Johnnie Drummond, the postman, beside his cycle shop in the Main Street, Callander, 1928.

Robert McLaren, dealer at Lagrannoch, *c.* 1920. Son of Robert McLaren the butcher. Meta Dow and George McAlpine look on.

The Callander Smithy, *c.* 1930. Here is Jackie Ferguson as a boy. Alaister McIntyre is shoeing the horse, Willie Henderson, the owner, is supervising, and Bob McLaren of Lagrannoch is the dealer.

The Waverley Hotel, *c.* 1920.

The Roman Camp Hotel, 1907. Built in the seventeenth century as a hunting lodge for the Duke of Perth.

The Palace Hotel. First built in 1881 as the Hydropathic Hotel, it burnt down in 1891. It was rebuilt only to burn down again, in 1895. Rebuilt yet again, it is thought that its name changed to the Palace Hotel around 1926. It eventually closed around 1950. The valuation roll for 1897 shows the owners as The Callander and Trossachs Hydropathic Co. Ltd.

The Lily Pond at the Palace Hotel.

St Kessog's church was built in 1883 by Robert Baldie of Glasgow. It was the parish church until 1929. In the foreground is the public war memorial, which was unveiled in 1921 by the Earl of Ancaster. Mr Archibald Kay, ARSA, RSW of Callander prepared the original sketch of the memorial. The architect was Mr A. McMichael, ARIBA and the monument is the work of Mr James Gray, Sculptor of the Glasgow School of Art. At Dounmhor, Callander, a cairn was erected in 1921 to the memory of former members of their local Boy Scouts. At that time Dr Beattie was the Scoutmaster and he helped the boys collect the stones from the Crags. The slab was the gift of Mr Collier, the builder, and Mr S. Copland did the lettering. The names recorded are Jimmy Liles, Archie MacDonald, Ian MacDonald, Leonard Skinner and Peter Stewart.

Ancaster Square and Tank *Julian*. A joint meeting of the Town and Parish Councils of Callander was held on 5 March 1918, and chaired by Provost MacDonald to discuss 'War Savings Week' in the town. The Committee agreed to aim at raising enough money as would be necessary to purchase a tank and an aeroplane. At a subsequent meeting on 30 July, Provost MacDonald announced that *Julian* the tank would visit Callander, and Lord Esher would be asked to assist the formal opening ceremony. The tank's visit was widely advertised and was aimed at promoting 'Save and Buy National War Bonds'. The above photograph shows *Julian's* visit to Callander on Wednesday 7 August 1918.

The Cycle Parade in Ancaster Square, 1924.

Cycle Parade, 1921. A popular event, the Cycle Parade usually took place during the Glasgow Fair Week. Every year the cyclists decorated their bicycles and paraded from one end of the town to the other before returning to the Square, where they were judged.

The Black Watch, during the First World War. From left to right, back row: Shankland, Duncan McArthur, James Hayes, -?-, David Irvine, Duncan Brown, -?-. Front: Alpine McAlpine, Robertson, Lt. David Calder, Duncan Ferguson, Colin Sinclair. Foreground: Edward McAlpine.

A group of nurses outside Inverleny House, Callander.

Inverleny House, Callander, in use as a military extension to Falkirk Infirmary during the First World War.

In 1923 the play at McLaren High School was *She Stoops To Conquer*. The actors are Norman Wilson and Crissie Stewart.

McLaren High and Callander Public School. The present day primary school occupies the original site of McLaren High School, built around 1892 by the McLaren Educational Trust and School Board. It moved to its present site in 1965.

Main Street looking east, *c.* 1920.

Main Street looking east, *c.* 1950.

The Old Bank House, No.3 Main Street, Callander. The Town Clerk had his office here. Prior to that, Walter Buchanan, a lawyer who was also the Town Clerk, occupied it. Part of No.1 is in the left of the photograph. This was the original Dreadnought Hotel. The 1873 Valuation Roll for No.3 shows the proprietor as Walter Buchanan, solicitor, and the tenant as Alexander Cameron, coachman.

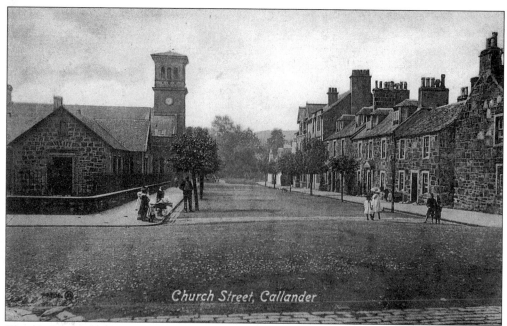

Church Street, 1910.

Callander United Free Church, *c*. 1913. Minister W.W. Gauld. On Sunday 15 May 1921, the then Minister, Revd R.E. McIntyre, MA unveiled three stained glass windows erected as a memorial to the twenty-five men of the congregation who fell during the First World War.

Callander Free Church Choir, October 1886. From left to right, back row: Thomas Hamilton (Kilmahog mill), Willie Robertson (The Lotts), Annie Thomson (married to William Ross, below), John McLean, John Vandyke, Peter McNiven, Mary McFarlane. Middle row: Lily Lumsden, John Brown, John Buchanan, John Anderson, Margaret Russell, John Smith, Mary McFarlane, James Haggart, Christian Douglas. Front row: William Ross, Jean Hamilton, Christina Stewart, Polly Cater (?), John Robertson, Isabella Buchanan, Gideon Collier.

Miss Margaret Stewart, Ancaster Square. Her father was Rob Stewart, the cattle dealer, who lived in a small cottage on Main Street. Her sister was Mrs P. Haggart (of Haggart's butchers) and she stayed with the Haggarts until her death. She is standing at the door of the Haggart's house, No.26.

Miss Betsy Mathison, 1969. She was the last crofter at Drumvaich.

Donald MacKay. One of four brothers, three of whom farmed the Mollands for over fifty years, Donald worked for MacFarlane's the carriers, delivering railway parcels. When this finished he went to work for the Council as the Callander Street cleaner.

Staff standing outside Lady Esher's house.

Alex Cram & Sons Bakers, Main Street. In the *Callander Advertiser* of May 1913, there was an advert publicizing the McLaren High School Sport's Day, with Messrs Cram & Sons providing refreshments and afternoon tea for 6d.

A postcard advertisement for Mr Wilson's tweed warehouse. This shop stood at the bottom of North Church Street and the corner of Main Street.

42

Showroom of Wm. Liles & Son, wallpaper suppliers, in Bridge Street.

Callander Institute FC, *c.*1926. From left to right, back row: William McIntyre, William Brown, Jonathan Callamin, John Duncanson, Bobby Campbell, Fergus Robertson. Front row: Tom McCaskill, Ian Henderson, Jim Bell, Alec MacKenzie, Stewart Colquhoun. Seated on the ground: George McDonald (son of the Institute caretaker).

Callander Thistle FC, 1916. From left to right, back row: William Brown (Trainer), John Bain, Ian Henderson, Alec Drummond. Middle row: William Haugh, Jim Bell, Jonathan Callamin, John Sutherland, Stewart Colquhoun. Front row: Colin McLaren, Tom McCaskill, John Campbell.

Angus McRae, champion piper, with Jock
Wilson, butler at the Roman Camp,
c. 1896.

1897. From left to right: Robert Strang, -?-, -?-, -?-, John Duncanson. Front: Dan McNiven, -?-,
(?) Adams. Adams was an insurance agent who lived who lived at 95 Main Street.

Ancaster Road, c. 1910.

The Wood Walk. An article in the *Callander Advertiser* of May 1913 stated that 'William Fletcher is currently laying out two extensions to the present walk. One, a continuation to the west leading to the top of the crags, and the other striking off about the middle of the present walk and also leading to the summit.'

The Queen's (Queen Victoria) Diamond Jubilee Cairn on the summit of Callander Crags, 1897. One of the men in the front row is the builder of the cairn, Malcolm Ferguson. This cairn was rebuilt in 1997.

Members of the Town Council and Shop Owners, 1899. From left to right, back row: John Johnson, -?-, John Henderson, -?-, -?-, Thomas Ritchie, Peter Henderson, -?-, -?-. Middle: -?-, -?-, W.B. Thomson, Alexander Stewart, James Gray, Duncan Stewart, William Freebain, Donald Campbell, Robert Fulton, Robert McLaren, -?-, John Ferguson, James Buchanan, Daniel Melrose. Front: (?) Robertson, -?-, John McLaren, Alexander Scott, John Davidson, A. Johnstone, Peter Robertson, Archibald McLaren, Alex Drysdale, -?-.

Bridgend, Callander. An idea of the diversity of the people and their trades can be gained from the 1851 Census. At No.3, Captain Andrew MacFarlan, Captain 91st Regiment of Foot, Half Pay. At No.7, John Buchanan, weaver. At No.8, Colin Buchanan, carter. At No.13, Donald McLaren, weaver. At No.14, John McFarlane, saddler. At No.15, Peter Strang, tailor. At No.16, Thomas Stewart, mason. At No.17, Robert Ferguson, cooper. At No.21, Robert McLaren, farm labourer.

Dreadnought Hotel. *Dreadnought* is the motto of the Clan MacNab, and it was the Chief of the Clan who built both the original hotel around 1810 (see page 37), and the Dreadnought Hotel, pictured here in 1920.

The view that now looks down over The Meadows car park.

The Leny Avenue, *c.* 1904.

Cottages at Kilmahog, *c*. 1909. There was once a saw mill in Kilmahog known as the 'pirn mill'. This mill's main output was bobbins of birch, mostly for the thread works of Messrs Coats in Paisley. The brush wood of the birch trees were made into brushes for street sweeping and sold to Glasgow and other cities. The mill was owned by Mr McLean, who also owned a grocery and provision shop in Upper Square, Callander. Mr McLean had trained in forestry and was practicing the many new methods of the time, one of which was using tree bark for tanning and dyeing. He employed a large number of men, and women and children were paid to peel bark from the oaks.

Kilmahog Village. In Gaelic, *Kilmachug*, meaning the 'Cell of St Hog' or 'St Chug'. The Festival of St Chug was celebrated on 26 March each year. In past times Kilmahog was the centre of a separate parish and had a larger population than Callander.

Kilmahog Village and the old Toll House.

Woodend, *c*. 1910.

Post Office van. On 31 January 1969, a post office van plunged into the River Leny, which was in spate. Luckily, the driver managed to open the door and escape to reach the bank safely.

Loch Lubnaig, Strathyre.

Road to Strathyre. In the distance on the right can be seen the chimney pots of Ardchullarie House. It was here that the great eighteenth century explorer, James Bruce, retired to write his account of his travels in Abyssinia. He set out to find the source of the Nile and travelled by foot to the source of the Blue Nile and into the heart of Abyssinia. After all his travels, which took him through the most inhospitable places, he died breaking his neck, falling down a flight of stairs whilst helping an old lady to her carriage at Kinnaird.

Three

Strathyre

Strathyre Station. The train arriving from Callander, *c.* 1960.

Strathyre Station, *c.*1898. At this time the stationmaster was John Sutherland. John Sutherland was born in Orkney in 1855 and was married to Jacobina Lumsden; they had a daughter Rachael, who went to the local school. He was stationmaster at Strathyre for forty-one years, and had only retired due to ill health two months prior to his death in Strathyre in September 1919. During his time at Strathyre, he kept the station looking beautiful. There is a stone erected in Balquhidder Churchyard by public subscription in appreciation of his faithful service. His wife died on 3 December 1944, aged ninety.

Strathyre Station, *c.*1910. Strathyre Station closed in 1965.

This photograph shows the fountain, which was awarded to Strathyre for the best kept station and now sits in the garden of Dunellan.

Station Hotel. Arriving from the train and looking out through the archway from the station towards the Station Hotel (now known as the Ben Sheann Hotel) must have been a lovely sight to behold and a real welcome to 'Bonnie Strathyre'. The photograph was taken around 1922, and to the right of this photograph is Immeriach. At one time, when the original hamlet of Strathyre called 'Stronyre' was at the other side of Loch Lubnaig, near Laggan Farm, it is thought that Immeriach was also a small hamlet situated near this spot. The birthplace, if you like, of Strathyre.

Buchanan Monument. To the right of this photograph stands a small monument to Dugald Buchanan, but many people walk by and have no idea of how great this man was. Dugald Buchanan was born in 1716 at Ardoch Mill, Strathyre. His father, John, had a small farm and mill near the Balvaig Burn. By the time Buchanan was twelve he was teaching the other children in the district. His father then sent him to the High Schools of Stirling and Edinburgh, and later he attended classes at Edinburgh University. His knowledge of the language was so brilliant that he was chosen to assist the Minister at Killin in translating the New Testament into Gaelic. He wrote some work in a volume of the Scottish History Society, dealing with the administration of fortified estates, and he published eight poems of *laoidhean spioradail* (spiritual hymns). Dugald also taught at the local schools here and was fourteen years the schoolmaster and evangelist at Kinloch Rannoch. Dugald Buchanan, poet, mystic, preacher, teacher and missionary, died of the plague in 1768.

Main Street, Strathyre, *c.* 1927. On the 1930 Valuation Roll, Donald McGregor owned Craigmore House, land, two houses and a byre. The first house next to the inn was listed as uninhabitable. The 1940 Valuation Roll shows a Miss Sarah Stewart living at Coire Buidhe.

The sign outside the Strathyre Inn, *c.* 1935.
Alexander Davidson was the innkeeper.
'Away ye gay landscapes' is the first line of
Byron's poem *Dark Lochnaigair*.

Strathyre Inn, *c.* 1932. This is when Alexander Davidson owned the inn.

The Studio, *c*. 1930. The pottery studio of Mary Ramsay and Jessie Wilson. Here we see Mary Ramsay (right) and possibly Jessie Wilson, outside the Studio. In this rare photograph you can see some of the pottery that could be purchased at the Studio. The pottery was painted and then transported up north to be fired, originally by Mary in her car, and then during the war years by Jessie on the train! The pottery that was produced at Strathyre is now quite valuable, and some pieces that were produced and signed by the artists can fetch over a hundred pounds today.

Here is another rare photograph of the Studio, *c*. 1930.

Mary Ramsay, *c.* 1934. The Ramsays lived at Dunnellan, Strathyre. Mary was born on 29 May 1896, her brother William in 1888. William was a writer and naturalist. Mary went to The Glasgow School of Art, where it is believed she met Jessie Wilson and Maggie MacDonald. Mary was a student between 1915 and 1919, while Maggie MacDonald was a student from 1910 to 1915. Later it is believed she produced some pottery at the Studio with Mary and Jessie. Jessie Wilson was a student from 1912 to 1917, and she specialised in embroidered cushions but also produced some pottery at the Studio. Between 1926 and 1928, Jessie Wilson and Mary were listed as tenants of the Studio. Jessie and Mary bought the studio in 1931. In later years the Studio passed to Mary's husband, Edgar King, and it became an antique shop.

The Strathyre Studio celebrates the Coronation of George VI with the rest of Strathyre.

Travelling people on their way to Callander, *c.* 1935, near the garage, Strathyre. It is believed the idea was to give money to the monkey and he then chose something for you from the back of the trap.

STRATHYRE FROM THE SOUTH.

This view around 1931 shows the old entrance to Tighness burn on the right, which runs under the bridge leading into Strathyre. At one time the public had access to this part of the burn and locals and travellers alike would take their horses to drink at this spot.

Tighness Bridge, Strathyre

This is the same as above but shows a clearer view of the access to the burn.

Immervoulin Farm, *c.* 1940. In 1891, Immervoulin was part of the of Baillie Hamilton Estate, and Henry Hill and his family lived there. In 1897 he was renting Immervoulin for £85. He also rented Kings House, Balquhidder between 1873 and 1897. He died in October 1900, aged eighty. In the 1930s, Peter Stewart was tenant followed by Jimmy Mackenzie. In 1964, Immervoulin was purchased by Cdr and Mrs Hutton, and was first used as a holiday cottage, then later as a riding and canoeing centre which reached its fame in the 1970s *Wish You Were Here* holiday TV programme. At one time Karen the eldest daughter was leading out three treks a day into the forests above Strathyre. Immervoulin is now owned by Cdr Tim Lloyds and has been developed into a touring caravan park, attracting thousands to the area each year.

Keip Farm c. 1930. Like Immervoulin across the river from Keip, this was also part of the Baillie Hamilton Estate. In 1851 there was a Peter McMartin aged sixty, living here with his wife Catherine, and at this time they were farming 200 acres of chiefly hill pasture. In 1873 the valuation roll shows Donald Cameron as head of the house. In 1891 Alex Cameron was head of the house. Between 1930 and 1940, Duncan Marques lived and farmed here. This photograph was taken prior to when the Blackburns came to live here in the late 1960s. In 1934 the Baillie-Hamilton Estate sold the farms and much of the land of Strathyre, totalling over 6,000 acres, to the Forestry Commissioners for £13,000.

Curling on Loch Lubnaig, *c.* 1930. The tall gentleman taking part is Ronnie Gibson, father of Ronnie and Jimmy. Ronnie originally came from St Andrews, then lived for a time at Strathlyn, Kilmahog, prior to coming to Strathyre and starting the garage. During the war he was a special constable and after the war became a JP (Justice of the Peace). The man with grey hair and a dark suit is believed to be Adam MacMorran, father of Willy MacMorran, a merchant in Strathyre in late 1960s.

Laggan Farm. This photograph outside Laggan shows Geraldine Gibson from Ardoch Cottage leaning against the car. South of Laggan lie the ruins of *Ardandamh* (meaning the height of the stag) which once belonged to the Fergussons. Laggan was also part of the of Baillie Hamilton Estate. James Stewart was head of the house in 1841 and according to census returns and valuation rolls it seems to have been farmed by that family until at least the 1930s.

Having a break at the sawmill near Immervoulin, *c.* 1950, are Fred Menzies and Bill Dye. Fred worked in the forestry for forty-four years. He is now retired but still living in Strathyre.

Donald Kennedy. This photograph shows Donald Kennedy at the Forestry Commission's nursery in Strathyre. Donald was one of a family of twelve from Glenogle, Lochearnhead. During the war years, Donald worked with the 'Land Girls', and after the war carried on working with the forestry. He was an incredibly kind man and full of fun. Donald's sister Mary still lives in Lochearnhead.

Outside the Nursery, Strathyre, in the late 1940s. From left to right: Willy Wright, Donald Kennedy, Jean Ferguson, -?-, Hugh Brown, Daisy Fisher, Lella Ferguson, Betty Sallie, Janet Brown, -?-, -?-.

Two German prisoners of war help Willy Macleod and Fred Menzies dig a deep drain for the back of the houses – *Elwyn*, *Tigh-meagham*, and *Mo- Dhachaidh*. These houses are all known now as Balvaig cottages and until recently they were all owned by the Forestry Commission.

The horse in the foreground was owned by John Grant – her name was *Rita* and she pulled the milkfloat. In the distance stands the original school building. On the left was the schoolhouse and on the right was the school.

Strathyre Primary School. This rare picture was taken around 1899 of the old Strathyre Primary School. The teacher was Miss Tocher, who originally came from the East of Scotland. Unfortunately, only one child can be named and that is Margaret Buchanan who is sitting on the extreme right of the front row. Earlier dates show that in 1851 a Robert Ferguson was living in the schoolhouse and in 1873 a teacher named Peter Colquhoun was living and teaching in Strathyre. Later, in 1891, Isabella Stewart (widow) was living in the schoolhouse with her unmarried daughter Harriet Stewart, who was the schoolmistress. Jumping ahead to around 1955, a Mrs Wilson was the teacher, followed for a short time by Mary McMorran and finally the last teacher of the old primary school, Mrs Dow, who also became the first teacher of the new school around 1959.

Ardoch House. This late 1930 photograph shows a very different Ardoch to the one we see today, which is much bigger than the original building.

The Temperance Hotel and the original shop, *c.* 1910. At one time there were two Temperance Hotels in Strathyre, the other one being the Munro. In 1897, Robert Stewart from Laggan was the owner of the Temperance and William Munro was the tenant. In 1873 the owner of the shop, now Ulva House, was Robert Stewart and the tenant was Duncan Fisher. Duncan Fisher was once on the valuation roll right through to 1897, and then in 1913 Mr Dewar was the merchant. In 1940 the owner of Ulva House was Adam McMorran, merchant (Adam's son William later took over the business). The shop then moved to the other side of the road were it remained right up until 1996, when a new shop was built. The owner and resident of Corriegowrie in 1873 was Robert Stewart and in 1930, James Stewart, boatman, was owner and occupier. In 1940, Corriegowrie had passed to Miss Janet Stewart.

Munro's Hotel, *c.* 1930. William Munro was a teacher and had been at one time schoolmaster and clerk to the board of Balquhidder. He was very knowledgeable about the district and was a widely-read man. He died on 22 April 1913, after a long illness. His funeral service took place at the hotel, conducted by the Revd Cameron, Balquhidder. After the service the coffin left the village on the 7.30 train to Inverness and then by coach to Glen Urquhart and the family burial ground. His estate, which was valued at £1,326 11s 5d, was passed to his wife Christina MacDonald Munro and his daughter Mary. His son in law took over the duties of hotelkeeper. In the valuation roll for 1940, Mary was listed as still being the owner of the hotel. Originally the Strathyre Temperance Hotel, then known later as Munro's Hotel, and now known as the Munro Hotel.

The old mill. This was next to *Tigh-Na-Shian* on the back road to Balquhidder.

Dochfour and Aldourie. The land that these houses are on was given to John Ferguson, weaver in Strathyre. He died in 1886 and it passed to Malcome Ferguson. When he died, the land was then part of Immeriach Barony of Strathyre. Duncan MacDonald then built the houses in 1901. Dochfour, which is on the left of the photograph, was sold in 1937 to Mrs Alice Gordon Sandiman or Wood, wife of Frank Watson Wood, artist of Bearsden. In 1940, Mary MacDonald, who also owned Rosebank, owned Aldourie. In 1947, Mary's brother John owned the house and sold it toWillimina MacDonald in 1948. In 1952, Aldourie was sold to Janette Marques Shena MacDonald Marques and Catherine Marques. In 1960, Curt and Susi Neustein moved in. Curt and Susi were Jewish, and before the war worked as furniture specialists. They had great knowledge of wood, and made chairs for the new German military academy. They left Germany after being warned of danger and escaped to the Dutch border with their children. After a few days they managed to get out, moving to Cornwall until after the war, when they re-located to Glasgow and then up to Aldourie. Subsequent moves later took the family to Balquhidder and on to London. Aldourie is now called Mandalay.

Rosebank, *c.* 1929. The proprietor of Rosebank House in 1897 was Duncan MacDonald, joiner, who built Aldourie and Dochfor, and he was still there until his death on 3 June 1936. His wife Janet died less than a year later in 1937. The house then passed to their daughter Mary Isabella MacDonald, whose brother in law was Duncan Marques of Keip Farm

Creagan, *c.* 1920. In 1851, Creagan was a 500 acre farm with fourteen acres arable. John Sanderson was the tenant and head of the house; he was a widower with two sons and a daughter, his son in law, sister in law and two grandchildren were all living in the house. This same family remained as tenants until 1897, when James his son was head of the house. In 1930, Duncan Stewart was tenant and Creagan was still owned by Mrs Baillie Hamilton.

Four
Balquhidder

Kingshouse Halt. The people of Balquhidder built Kingshouse Halt in 1871. In 1871 the railway was short of funds but they agreed to stop the trains if the people of Balquhidder paid for the station, which they did. Later, the locals asked if the platform could be extended, and this was agreed if the timber could be supplied free of charge. Again, this was duly done, but the locals were later refused by the railway company when asked if the company would carry a mailbag.

Kingshouse Hotel. This hotel was built in 1747 as a resting-place for the use of drovers on the way to the cattle markets at Crieff and Falkirk. This was once the site of a military barracks and a mail and coach halt.

Kingshouse Hotel. Kingshouse was part of the Baillie-Hamilton Estate and there are records which mention Ewan Cameron as innkeeper and farmer at Kingshouse around 1840-1850. Henry Hill, of Immervoulin, Strathyre, was farmer and innkeeper here too from around 1873-1900. Henry Hill was believed to have married twice. A very well known farmer at the markets of Crieff, Falkirk, Oban, Mull and Fort William, he was a shrewd businessman. His wife kept the inn going in her husband's absence and Robert Louis Stevenson stayed at the Kingshouse whilst she was there, writing his notes for *Catriona* and *Kidnapped*. Henry Hill eventually died in October 1900.

This postcard is captioned 'The Braes of Balquhidder', which is not strictly true, as the 'Braes' start further up from approximately Kirkton Glen. The view here is pre railway – up on the top right is Auchtubh and slightly to the left is Coshnachie; the Smithy is to the far left. There are records that say a Culdee monastery existed about one and a half miles north west of Kingshouse. *Balquhidder* means 'a village upon which five glens are seen' or 'a village at the centre of five glens'.

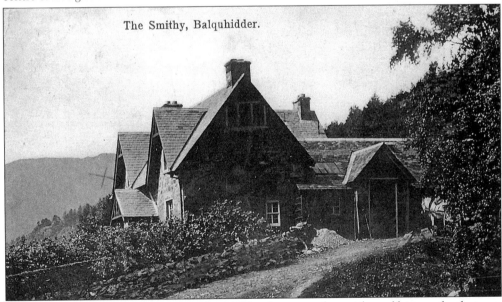

The Smithy, *c.* 1910. In 1897, Alexander McNaughton was the smith, and his rent for that year was £6 to David Carnegie of Stronvar. Alexander was born in Crieff, and his wife Mary was born in Balquhidder. They had two sons, Duncan and Alex, and a daughter Mary. Duncan, his son, was later to become the last smith in Balquhidder; he was also the session clerk, church organist, registrar of births, deaths and marriages, and poor law inspector. He died in 1951 a well-loved and respected man.

The Village, Balquhidder, Perthshire.

Kirkton Inn. This was once Keeper's Cottage and before that Stewart's Alehouse, where Rob Roy would visit for his noggin. In the days of the Carnegies the keeper lived here and from here ponies carrying fish would be taken up the Kirkton Glen to restock the lochs.

The Post Office, Balquhidder. (No. 245.)

The Post Office. Way back in time this was a lint mill once known as Weaver's Cottage, home of Duncan McAlpine, a joiner from Stronvar who, as a hobby, made violins. When Duncan died, his wife ran the Post Office from home. Later, after she died, the Post Office moved across the road to a new building built by the Carnegies.

74

Kirkton Farm, *c.* 1920.

Kirkton Highland Games. Crianlarich School competing in Balquhidder at the original Lochearnhead games. These games were sponsored by the Edinchip Sports Club and put forward by Hugh MacDiarmid. The games were strictly amateur and not for the tourist trade. Called The Balquhidder, Lochearnhead and Strathyre Games, they were run by five people and rotated between the villages. The games stopped just short of the Second World War.

The School, Balquhidder

905

The School. The new school building was built around 1860 and closed in 1994. The old school building was up at the top of the church brae (on the bank) and above the road close to the churchyard wall. John Carleton was schoolmaster in 1841. This photograph of the new school is taken about 1920. The school closed after the roll had dropped each year until there were only two pupils left: Clair Marshall and Suzanne Doyle.

Balquhidder schoolchildren, c. 1960, with the then head teacher Miss Stewart on the left, and Betty Beauchamp, who later went on to become head teacher, on the far right. From left to right, back row: John Jackson, David Robertson, Joan Fergusson, Maclure, Caroline Renshaw, Janet Jackson, Gillian Perks, Jean Moir, Janice Fergusson, John Thow. Middle: Robert Allison, Walter Anderson, David Thow, Donald Saunders, Helen Renshaw, William Massie, Margaret Massie. Front: Quintus Renshaw, Kirk Saunders, Ewan MacGregor, Duncan MacDiarmid, Billy Fergusson, Margaret MacDiarmid, Andrew Matygasek, Sandie Massie, Betty Massie, Joy Robertson, Robin Matygasek, Kenneth.

Miss World, Miss Grenada with Betty Beauchamp, the head teacher of Balquidder Primary School, on a visit in 1971. Jennifer Hoskin (Miss Grenada) had a great grandmother who was a MacGregor from Aberdeen. A stamp was later issued in Grenada, depicting Jennifer Hoskin and Rob Roy MacGregor.

War memorial and old church. It is believed that Christianity was first brought to Balquhidder by St Angus, possibly in the seventh or eighth century. St Angus lived near the river at Kirkton and was buried on the hill which overlooks Kirkton. Eventually a small church named *Eaglais Beag* was built over the site of his grave. In 1631, Lord Scone built a church partly on top of the pre-Reformation church, and at one time the walls could be seen in the area around Rob Roy's grave.

Rob Roy's Grave. Rob Roy was baptised on 7 March 1671. His father was Lt Col. Donald MacGregor of Glengyle, the chieftain of his clan and a Jacobite. His mother, Margaret Campbell, was a half-sister of Campbell of Glen Lyon, who directed the massacre at Glencoe. Starting out in life as a cattle dealer, Rob's exploits are well documented. He married Mary MacGregor, daughter of Gregor MacGregor of Carnermore. Rob died on 28 December 1731 at Inverlochlarig.

The marriage of William Ramsay (Strathyre) and Christina MacNaughton (Balquhidder). Mary Ramsay is standing second from the left, between the other two MacNaughton sisters. To the right of William Ramsay is possibly his brother, George.

The present church was built by David Carnegie of Stronvar and was opend in September 1855. The architect was David Bryce.

Glen Buckie. Glen Buckie is steeped in history and has seen some famous footsteps pass this way. The ordinary working folk walked through on their way to the markets along with the women and children from the farms below, who brought the animals up to the summer dwellings, 'the sheilings', for the summer months. .

Bailefuill. Set in some beautiful scenery on the back road between Strathyre and Balquhidder, Bailefuill was once a farm and is now an outdoor centre.

This photograph was taken about 1935. The location has not been identified.

Haymaking at Auchleskine, Balquhidder, c. 1895.

Stronvar House, Balquhidder. David Carnegie put his mark on the area of Balquhidder. He drained the land and built many buildings including Stronvar House, Balquhidder church, and the school. He also established gardens and employed many workers, both local and those who lived on the estate. When David Carnegie died in 1890 at the age of seventy-seven, he left an estate valued at £500,000. His eldest son James and his wife Mary took over the running of the estate with vigour, Mary even going as far as naming the children on the estate! There were three dances a year held at Stronvar, and Christmas parties for tenants and children. James Carnegie died in 1925 aged seventy-eight, and Mary in 1938 aged ninety-two.

James Fergusson and possibly his brother John, clipping up at Tuarach, c. 1915.

Filling up the sacks with the wool .The wool would be tied into rolls then packed into bags. The smaller children would get the job of getting into the sacks and pushing the wool into the corners! The sacks were filled so they were lovely and smooth with not a bump in sight. In this photograph the bag is being sewn up.

THE BLACK ISLAND,
BALQUHIDDER.

The Black Island Stronvar, 1915. Up at the back of Stronvar House is a walk up a path that leads into Glen Buckie. This path carries on up to a mill that stands alongside the Calair burn. At one time this could be reached by this little bridge and is marked on the Ordnance Survey map of 1866. This was one of many bridges that Mrs Carnegie had erected around this area, but alas the bridge is no longer there.

Monachyle Hostel once stood six miles from Balquhidder between Loch Voil and Loch Doine.

Balquhidder School, c. 1952. From left to right: John Littlejohn, Ewan Stewart, Donnie and Anne Campbell, Finlay Gordon, Robin Turnbull, Catriona Fergusson, Maisie Stewart, John MacDiarmid, Kathleen Mckay, Iseabal Fergusson.

Inverlochlarig, *c.* 1935.

Mrs Bethune Carnegie, 1905.

BALQUHIDDER.

Near Balquhidder Station, c.1930. The owner of the shop in 1930 was Duncan McLaren from Glasgow, and the tenant was James Twaddle, merchant. This building is now the Golden Larches Restaurant. The railway closed in 1965 and Balquhidder lost its station.

Near the station, Balquhidder. (No. 316.)

Taken near the station, Helensfield is on the left of the photograph.

Five

Lochearnhead

Lochearnhead School, 1910. The headmaster was Dominie MacDonald, whose wife was the sister of the novelist Annie S. Swan. The teacher was Miss Pollock. From left to right, back row: Miss Pollock, -?-, -?-, Albert Stewart Ardvolich (walked three and a half miles to school each day!), -?-, Alex MacIntosh, Hugh McDiarmid, -?-, Dominie MacDonald. Middle: -?-, -?-, -?-, -?-, Kate Livingston, Annie Munro(?), -?-, Cathy MacGregor. Front: Douglas McLaren (his father was once gamekeeper at Edinkeip), Kate McLaren, Peggy McLaren (became a nurse), Isa Thorton (daughter of the postmaster), Teany Cameron (her father owned Letters Farm), Peggy MacDonald (daughter of Dominie MacDonald), Jenny MacGregor, -?-, Duncan MacIntire.

Entrance to Lochearnhead, *c.* 1900. In 1897 the old Post Office (now the village shop) was owned by the Lady Helen Laura MacGregor. The postmaster was William Thornton, the postman was Alexander McDonald and the postrunner was Hugh McEwan. William Thornton's father, Henry, was born in Girvan, Ayrshire and spent eleven years working at the Department of Ordnance Survey. When the Callander & Oban Railway was about to be constructed, Henry Thornton measured and laid out the line between Callander and Dalmally. He then became postmaster at Lochearnhead for thirty-two years until, after a week's serious illness, he died on 2 February 1895 at the age of sixty-three.

The Episcopal church, *c.* 1915.

This postcard is dated 1937, and the message reads on the back reads: 'This is the slickest bar ever.'

This postcard is dated 1924 and is written by Vera Holme, who describes herself as living in the 'little house in the middle of this picture called *Tigh Na Gich*.'

The Auld Gean Tree. A cherry tree, it was a focal point for young people to meet in the evening. This tree was blown down in a gale and another was later planted by Donald Kennedy for Sir Malcome MacGregor.

Mountain Climbing Club on the slopes of Ben Vorlich. Hugh McDiarmid (far right) with Duncan Fraser, Allan McIntyre and John MacLaren. Duncan Fraser lost a leg in the Second World War, and later had a job as a watchman at Glen Ogle, watching for rockfalls and warning trains. John MacLaren was a very clever man who, due to the economic situation at this time, worked as a porter at Balquhidder Station.

Lochearnhead School, 1896. Lochearnhead School celebrated its Centenary in 1996. An ordnance survey map of 1867 shows a Free Church school on this site. At that time there was also another school situated on the way into Lochearnhead, opposite the old Post Office.

Here is a picture of many old friends at Lochearnhead School in 1961. From left to right, back row: Marie King, Neil Kennedy, Jessica Prentice, Lachie MacGregor, Sandra Geddes, Michael Hapka, Janet Geddes, Third row: -?-, Rhoda MacGregor, Elaine Cameron, Angus MacDiarmid, Mairi Kennedy, Gillian McLauchlan, Caroline Boscowan. Second row: John Duncan, Peter Szuszkewicz, Rosemary Brown, William Szuszkewicz, Anne Johnston, Allan Prentice, Sheena Bryson, Ian Johnston. Front: C.Geddes, Kenny McLachlan, Rona McLachlan, Gerald Brown, Marie Brown, Charles Finney, Alison Geddes.

Tea Room and Fir Avenue, *c*. 1930. Known as both the 'Tea Room' and the 'Coffee Shop', it supplied refreshments to locals, tourists and carters. This building later became the Village Hall. The 1930 Valuation Roll states: 'Site for Coffee House. D. L. Morton per Jenkins and Jardine, Solicitors, Stirling. Occupier: Lady MacGregor of MacGregor.' This postcard, taken shortly after this date, has a message stating that the lady had supper here.

The Auchraw Hotel. Built by John MacGregor of Craigroyston in the 1920s. Its name was changed to the Marie Stewart, and after lying empty for around ten years it was pulled down in 1995.

Play at Lochearnhead. Hugh McDiarmid can be seen on the extreme left at the top of the photograph.

The road out of Lochearnhead to St Fillans.

Cottages, c. 1900. Present location unknown.

Local fiddlers, *c.* 1936. From left to right: Ronnie Gibson, Hugh McDiarmid, Jimmy Fergusson and Constable Sam Allan.

The *Queen of Lochearn*. This steamer ran during the summer months from St Fillans to Lochearnhead and made two trips a day. It was owned by the Alexander Bus Company and ran until the Second World War. In the distance is Edinample Castle.